the DANCE

Keeping in step with the King

Jan Mozingo & Angie Buhrke

The Dance

Copyright © 2025 Jan Mozingo & Angie Buhrke

ISBN # 978-1-966448-19-8

All rights reserved. No part of this publication may be reproduced or transmitted in any form or by any means without written permission from the publisher.

Unless otherwise noted, all Scriptures are taken from the *Modern English Version* of the Bible. Copyright © 2014 by Military Bible Association. Published and distributed by Charisma House.

Scripture quotations marked TPT are from The Passion Translation®. Copyright © 2017, 2018, 2020 by Passion & Fire Ministries, Inc. Used by permission. All rights reserved. ThePassionTranslation.com.

Contact Information for Jan Mozingo: reviveusnow.com

Contact Information for Angie Buhrke: info@victorylifeministries.org

Editor: Ginny van Gulick

Cover Design: Josh Ferguson, Sermon Box

Layout: Satoshi Yamamoto

Printed in the United States of America

Table of Contents

Acknowledgments i

Foreword iii

Introduction v

Part 1: Jan Mozingo

Chapter 1—The Dance 3

Chapter 2—The Importance of Unity 7

Chapter 3—From the Beginning 15

Chapter 4—Recognizing the Drift 19

Chapter 5—Why? 25

Chapter 6—Called to Make a Difference 31

Chapter 7—Let's Enter In 35

Part 2: Angie Buhrke

Chapter 8—Hopscotch Christianity 41

Chapter 9—New You = New View 45

Chapter 10—Backward Thinking 51

Chapter 11—Your Thoughts 57

Chapter 12—Switch Your Thinking! 65

Chapter 13—The Creative Power of Words 71

Chapter 14—Actions of Honor 77

Chapter 15—The Proof Is in the Doing 81

Chapter 16—In Step with the King 89
Prayer to Receive Jesus as Your Lord and Savior 91
Prayer to Receive the Baptism of the Holy Spirit 93
Suggested Readings 97

Acknowledgments

We want to thank our Lord and Savior, Jesus Christ, for His love and faithfulness, for personally revealing the truths within this book, and for cheering us on while writing it.

Thank you to Satoshi Yamamoto for, once again, creating an outstanding interior design and layout.

Thank you to my friend, Ginny van Gulick for her superb editing.

Thanks to Josh Ferguson of Sermon Box for his awesome cover design and for all he does for Victory Life Ministries.

Thanks to Pastor Todd Mozingo for the Foreward.

Foreword

You can ignore it if you like, but that does not make it go away. You can choose not to discuss it, but that does not make it better. You can condemn it without a solution and all you have done is contribute to the problem. What are we talking about? Division. Not a difference of opinion or a misinterpretation, but division; sometimes covert and sometimes intentional, that is never really understood or recognized by most Christians. It permeates so many areas of our walk with Christ, with each other and with the Holy Spirit. It is a subtle tool that the enemy seeds so that we in turn have a lack of desire to fully grow into what we are called to be.

The answer? Unity. True, legitimate unity in the Holy Spirit. As believers, we are called to keep in step with the Lord, walking in harmony with His will and His Word. Yet too often, we stray into our own paths, led by personal agendas, preferences, or traditions, rather than the Spirit of Christ. This misalignment is the root of much division, because unity can only exist where we are all following the same Leader. God makes it very clear that unity is critical in the bride of Christ. How can you dance with someone and not be in unity with them?

Jan Mozingo and Angie Buhrke are both senior, experienced leaders in the Body of Christ. They do not play games, and they do not write frivolous words on a page to placate the desire to publish a book. They have watched the schemes of the enemy and the lack of understanding in the church. They have both seen the destruction that division causes. Jan and Angie are well equipped with discernment and the discerning of spirits so that they can bring into the light the cunning works of our enemy. So, they have taken on the challenge of explaining division and unity through The Dance. What a perfect picture of operating in unison to accomplish something beautiful.

Get ready to let the revelation of this book open your eyes to the often intimate, fulfilling and flowing unison of the dance offered by the Holy Spirit.

Pastor Todd Mozingo
Revive Church
Stuart, Fl.

Introduction

The Christian life is often described as a walk, but sometimes, it's more like a dance. A dance speaks of rhythm, relationship, and movement. The question is: whom are we dancing with?

God has invited us to move in step with Him by being led by His Word, guided by His Spirit, and rooted in His truth. But in the noise of culture, opinions, and distractions, it's easy to find ourselves out of rhythm. Without even realizing it, we may start dancing to a different tune.

For example, whenever my husband hears a song, he instinctively starts tapping along. He's usually offbeat—tapping to his own rhythm instead of the actual music. Frankly, it's hard to listen to, but funny at the same time. It's also a picture of how we can live our faith. We think we're in rhythm with God, but we're really just following our own beat.

The Dance

Sometimes, we dance with the world, letting its values shape our decisions. Sometimes, we dance with our own opinions, putting personal comfort above biblical truth. Sometimes, we even dance with fear, doubt, or distraction, stepping away from the clarity and peace God offers. And sometimes, we try to dance with everyone at once, leading to confusion and division in the body of Christ. But there's good news: God is still holding out His hand.

This book is a call back to the original dance, one of unity, clarity, and purpose. It's about recognizing where we've stepped off track, and how we find joy again in realigning with God's view. When we move with Him, we move in peace, in truth, and in unity with one another.

Let's rediscover the beauty of dancing with the One who leads perfectly. Let's choose the one view that brings us together—His.

Angie

PART 1

Jan Mozingo

Chapter 1

The Dance

When you hear the word dance, what comes to mind? Maybe it's the twirl of a ballroom waltz, elegant and smooth, gliding across polished floors. Perhaps it's the energy of the twist, a line dance, breakdance, a community moving in step, all in sync. Or the passion of the tango, the intensity of the rumba, the bounce of a polka, each with its own rhythm, its own meaning, its own story.

Dance can be beautiful, synchronized, and cooperative. Two partners moving as one, anticipating each other, complementing each other. But sometimes, dance can also be chaotic, filled with tension. Two forces, constantly shifting, pulling away, pushing together, never quite settling, yet still moving to the same music. We can feel that kind of dance not just on the dance floor, but in the air. In the atmosphere around us.

The Dance

There's a dance happening in our world today. It's a dance of division and unity, of peace and conflict. We see it in politics. Country against country, nation against nation. We remember history's rhythms, north versus south, now red versus blue. We see it in families—parents and children pushing and pulling through growth and misunderstanding, marriages that flow like a graceful waltz, while others spiral like opposing storms locked in battle.

We even see it in the church. Groups within the body of Christ moving in opposite directions, each claiming to walk in the Spirit, yet heading down completely different paths. Two people both calling themselves Christians, but in times of elections their beliefs and moral decisions are polar opposites. What a paradox. Unity declared, division displayed.

We see it with Catholic and Protestant, Baptist and Pentecostal, doctrine and practice, Spirit and flesh, conviction and grace. We feel the tension, the rhythm of disagreement trying to move to the music of God's love. Some dances are smooth. Others are jagged. But either way, we're always dancing.

Every day, in every relationship, in every community and church, we dance. Sometimes toward God's kingdom.

The Dance

Sometimes away from it. And sometimes, we don't even realize which direction we're headed. But God set us up to dance with Him and in harmony with each other.

Recently I had the joy of spending time with my sister on a cruise. It was an awesome time of celebrating so many great things happening within our country and within our personal lives. On that ship, we danced every chance we could get. We were in sync. It's a beautiful thing when we are in harmony with one another. There can be differences, for sure, but coming in sync with one another in spite of a few differences is wonderful. So much joy!

Unfortunately, what I see within the body of Christ is much division. There's a heartbreaking discord. People don't realize they've stepped off the dance floor of the Kingdom and onto one that belongs to the world. They think they're dancing with the Lord, but their movements follow the rhythm of the flesh, the culture, or even the whispers of the enemy.

It's subtle at first. A misstep here. A turn that feels right, but pulls them in the wrong direction. The music shifts, and instead of listening for God's tempo, they start moving to a different beat. One that promotes self over surrender, pride over humility, control over trust. We are all given the opportunity, daily, to choose how we'll dance. Will we move in step with the Spirit or stumble in the flesh?

Galatians 5 tells us plainly to "walk by the Spirit, and you will not gratify the desires of the flesh." But walking or dancing with the Spirit isn't automatic. It's intentional. It's a decision we make with every breath, every reaction, every conversation. And this isn't a solo dance. We don't live in isolation. Our rhythm affects those around us—our families, churches, coworkers, and communities. When we're out of step with God, it causes friction. Disunity. Confusion. But when we're all dancing in sync with the Spirit, there's a harmony that can only come from heaven.

The dance of the Kingdom isn't about perfect moves. It's about surrendered ones. Some of the greatest dancers in God's eyes aren't the ones who twirl flawlessly, but the ones who stop mid-step and say, "Lord, I've lost the beat—help me find it again." This is where we start, recognizing the choice in front of us. The Spirit or the flesh. The Kingdom or the world. Unity or division. Love or pride. We're all dancing. The question is: whom are you dancing with?

Chapter 2

The Importance of Unity

It was early Monday morning in October 2024 when I heard the voice of the Lord clearly say, "This is the season of the dance." I knew exactly what it meant, and I knew where it was coming from. Yes, it was a big election year, and that carried its own weight, but this was bigger than politics. It was deeper. It was everything. I felt it in my bones.

This wasn't the first time I'd heard words regarding the dance, but something was different this time. This was the season to talk about it, to declare it. So I went to work, and as soon as I could, I started jotting down every detail the Lord was showing me. I began to see it everywhere, every situation, every movement, every turn of life felt like part of a dance.

There are times when others struggle to see what I see, to catch the rhythm I hear in the spirit. But shortly after that word came to me, others began to share the same things—visions, impressions, confirmations. It always seems to work that way, doesn't it? Being a pastor's wife, I'm so grateful to be part of a spiritual church where we are free to move in the Spirit, where we expect to hear from God, where we can trust that if He gives a word to one, He will confirm it through others.

Along with those words came a vision. I saw thousands of believing ladies dancing their own dance. I wondered and asked the Lord how we could be all over the place in the things we believe and are fighting for? How could we be so divided when it comes to the truth? There was simply no unity.

Everywhere I look, it feels like we're surrounded by division. I remember the days of Covid, so much loss, so many deaths, schools shutting down, travel halted, even churches closed. Families were torn apart by differing views, communities fractured, and entire countries felt the strain. And now, the wars in Gaza and Ukraine continue to deepen global divides, while protests, riots, and the persecution of Christians and Jews add to the unrest. Inflation keeps rising, making everyday life even harder. It's like the world is breaking apart at every level, politically, socially, and spiritually.

It's understandable that the world is divided. Without Christ, there's no true peace or unity. But what's more troubling is that same division is found among Christians. We are called to be united in Christ, set apart from the chaos, shining as a light in a world that desperately needs Jesus.

Unity within the Church, is not necessarily agreeing on worship styles or personal callings, but in the foundational truths we believe and stand on. It's one thing to serve God in different ways, some teach, some sing, some serve quietly behind the scenes, but at the core, we're meant to be united in truth. That's where our power as the Body of Christ really begins to show.

When we're like-minded, believing the same Gospel, standing on the same Word, seeking the same Spirit, we move as one. And when we move as one, God's will gets done. There's clarity, strength, and a tangible presence of the Spirit. But when we're divided over foundational truths, it hinders everything. Here are a few scriptures that have been speaking to me about this:

The Dance

1. 1 Corinthians 1:10:

> *Now I ask you, brothers, by the name of our Lord Jesus Christ, that you all speak in agreement and that there be no divisions among you. But be perfectly joined together in the same mind and in the same judgment.*

Paul wasn't asking for surface-level unity here. He was calling believers to be united in mind and thought. That doesn't mean we lose individuality, but it does mean we align our minds with Christ and our thoughts with Scripture. We can't afford to be splintered in doctrine and vision.

2. Ephesians 4:3-6:

> *…be eager to keep the unity of the Spirit in the bond of peace. There is one body and one Spirit, even as you were called in one hope of your calling, one Lord, one faith, one baptism, one God and Father of all, who is above all, and through all, and in you all.*

Unity takes effort. It's not passive, it's intentional. We protect unity by focusing on the "one faith," not letting secondary issues divide us. There is one Spirit we're following.

If we're listening to Him, we won't be pulled in different directions.

3. John 17:20-23 (Jesus praying):

> *"I do not pray for these alone, but also for those who will believe in Me through their word, that they may all be one, as You, Father, are in Me, and I in You. May they also be one in Us, that the world may believe that You have sent Me. I have given them the glory which You gave Me, that they may be one even as We are one: I in them and You in Me, that they may be perfect in unity, and that the world may know that You have sent Me, and have loved them as You have loved Me."*

Jesus Himself prayed for our unity, not just for our sake, but so the world would believe. Disunity among believers can actually become a stumbling block for others coming to Christ. Unity isn't just a nice idea, it's a testimony to the power and reality of Jesus.

4. Philippians 2:1-2:

> *If there is any encouragement in Christ, if any comfort of love, if any fellowship of the Spirit, if any*

compassion and mercy, then fulfill my joy and be like-minded, having the same love, being in unity with one mind.

Being united with Christ should lead to being united with each other. Like-mindedness isn't about opinions, it's about heart and mission. It's about loving with the same love Christ showed us. When you are like-minded, and are going in the same direction, there is unity and things go smoothly. This is what's supposed to happen within the Body of Christ. Since planting Revive Church, we've been incredibly blessed to experience a strong sense of unity, and even though challenges come, they've been few and far between because we've made it a priority to walk in love and stay grounded in truth.

We don't have to all look the same, sound the same, or serve in the same way. But when it comes to our foundation, who Jesus is, what He's done, and the truth of the Gospel, we must be aligned. The early church was powerful not because they had perfect people, but because they were devoted to the apostles' teaching, to prayer, and to each other (Acts 2:42-47). They were of one accord, and that's when the Holy Spirit moved mightily.

The Importance of Unity

If we want to see God's will done on earth as it is in heaven, we need to walk in step together, not just side by side, but heart to heart and mind to mind, united in truth.

Chapter 3

From the Beginning

Eden. A beautiful garden created for Adam and Eve. They spent time with God in the cool of the day. I can just imagine the refreshment, the conversation, all the questions they must have had. The beautiful intimacy. A divine dance.

Can you imagine how clean and refreshed they felt conversing with the God of the universe, asking Him about each plant and creature, sampling all the fresh fruits He created for them? I'm guessing they could have relaxed in the thick, tall grass under a beautiful palm, enjoying the water, with their long hair waving in the breeze, the sun shining golden streaks along their tanned bodies, and everything in front of them. Relaxed. Safe. Secure. Together. Intimacy with their God and each other. Not a worry or care in the world!

The Dance

Slowly the moon rises as the stars begin to sparkle and they drift to sleep. Another beautiful day in the perfect garden, followed by sweet dreams as they rest, refresh, and fully prepare for another perfect day in the perfect garden. The perfect dance.

This goes on for days, weeks, months, and years. Watching life grow, receiving a perfect harvest while watching your favorite plants, animals, and flowers grow. The dance continues. But one day everything changes. Suddenly there's a distraction from the peace. A voice not familiar. *"Did God really say...?"* A question from the outside. Has he been there all along and waited for just the right time to appear?

That moment of doubt, of questioning what they knew deep down to be true, was the first misstep. And once they took that step out of rhythm, everything changed. They stopped moving with the Father and started moving to the sound of another voice. Confusion entered. Deception followed. And soon, shame took the place of intimacy.

Suddenly things felt darker than ever before. Guilt, shame, and embarrassment. They wanted to hide. Fear and anxiety. They switched dance partners. But, their best

Friend, their most intimate dance partner, went looking for them, and all they could do was hide. Their emotions were overwhelming. They realized it was too late. They would never be the same.

What had been peace turned into hiding. What had been clarity became clouded with fear. The dance was broken, not because God changed, but because they turned their hearts away from His Word. And I can't help but see the same pattern still playing out today.

God has given us His Word, His Spirit, His presence. But the enemy still whispers: "Did God really say…?" And if we're not grounded, if we start entertaining those questions instead of standing on what we know is true, we'll step out of sync.

That's why it's so important that we align ourselves daily with God, not with culture, not with our emotions, and definitely not with the lies of the enemy. God's Word must be our foundation. Not just something we read, but something we live. Something we obey.

We were created for unity with God. For fellowship, for closeness. And out of that sweet unity, we stay in step

The Dance

with Him. We choose what's right, even when it's hard. We trust His Word, even when we don't understand. And we reject every voice that contradicts His truth. Because there's only one voice that leads to life. Every other voice leads us back to hiding.

So today, let's realign. Let's come back into rhythm. Let's trust Him fully again. Because the dance is still open, and He's still calling us to move with Him.

Chapter 4

Recognizing the Drift

Here are a few examples of what it looks like to leave the divine dance with Jesus, those moments when we let go of His hand and choose to follow another lead. These are the quiet compromises, the subtle shifts, the choices that seem small but speak loudly. They reveal the ways we stop moving in step with His Word and start dancing to the rhythm of deception instead.

Was there a time when you were in sync with the Lord fulfilling His plan for you? But then you heard a whisper. It wasn't loud. It wasn't obvious. It was just a suggestion. It was more of a thought that you were missing something, and you paused for a moment? It's at that moment of pause when you began to let go of His hand. You received the suggestion made to you and chose to dance with that lie.

It could be anything. Have you listened to the lie of the enemy when he tells you that you're not enough and that you'll never measure up? You're dancing with insecurity covered in shame. You try harder, work longer, read and pray more, but nothing can shake that lie that you're just not good enough for God. It's a never-ending cycle of self-righteousness, combined with guilt and shame. But the Bible says in 2 Corinthians 5:21 that we were made the righteousness of God, but you ignore the truth and believe a lie.

Have you been hurt? We all have at some point in our lives, but it's what we do with that hurt that's important. For example: someone offends you and you replay it in your mind feeding the anger and justifying your resentment. You repeat the offense to whomever will listen, which is allowing the bitterness to grow. The enemy keeps you bound in your unforgiveness. But the Bible says in Ephesians 4:32 that we are to forgive others just as God forgave us. Holding on to offense may not look like rebellion, but it's one of the quietest ways to let go of God's hand. Rather than moving in step with His grace, we freeze in bitterness. Out of God's love for us should flow forgiveness to others.

Do you check in with social media where you see the life of others, their body, their success, their husband?

You may have become envious and start to question God's goodness to you. That's the enemy whispering, "God's holding out on you." The Bible tells us in Galatians 5:19-20 that envy is a work of the flesh. Your flesh is opposite of the Spirit of God, and we are all given the free will and ability to operate in the Spirit or in the flesh. The choice is ours. Envy is your way of saying to God, "I'm not happy with Your plan for me. I want more from You. I want a bigger house, a nicer car, and more vacations." There's nothing wrong with these things unless they have a hold on you. Your lusting after these things is another sign of agreeing with the enemy that your needs aren't met the way you want them met. You're out of step.

How about saying "yes" when your heart says "no." You would rather offend God than disappoint people. You crave approval like it's oxygen. You are dancing with fear of man rather than resting in the Father's love for you. The Bible says in Galatians 1:10 that true servants of Christ do not seek approval of men. Christ already approves of us and that should be enough.

What about voting, which is a big one for me personally. When it comes to voting, it's not just a political act. It's a spiritual one. Many Christians vote with their emotions, fears, or preferences. We elevate charisma over character. We prioritize policies that benefit us, even if they dishonor God's Word. We say we want righteousness in the land, but we support those who mock it. We talk about freedom, but vote for bondage. We've left the divine dance and chose to dance with the enemy. The Bible says in 1 Corinthians 11:1 that we are to be imitators of Christ. Christians should be voting based on the individual who is most closely aligned with Scripture. They don't have to be perfect, but your candidate of choice should somewhat imitate the character of Jesus.

Many Christians numb themselves from their pain through addiction such as, alcohol, drugs, excessive buying, or sexual compromise. Anything to quiet the ache. Instead of bringing your pain to the Healer, you let the enemy offer you temporary relief. He'll numb your pain, so he can numb your purpose. But the Bible tells us in Exodus 15:26 that God is your Healer. Run to Him, not from Him, and receive all that He has for you.

These aren't just moral failures, they're missed steps in the dance. But the beauty of grace is this: the moment you realize whom you're dancing with, you can stop and turn back. The Father is always near, hand outstretched, ready to take the lead again.

Chapter 5

Why?

So why do we leave our dance partner, Christ, and turn to the world or even to the enemy? Just to be clear, we are not leaving Christ, our Lord and Savior. We are not losing our salvation or giving our lives over to the enemy. What it does mean is that in our daily lives we sometimes get distracted. We move in and out of what God wants us to do. We don't always stay in step with Him. But He is always there, still holding out His hand, ready for us to return to the dance.

There are several reasons why we change dance partners. One major reason is that we don't truly know who we are in Him. We forget our identity as sons and daughters of God. We don't fully grasp what God has done for us, that we've been saved completely—past, present, and future—and forgiven, not just partially, but entirely. Yet we still live like we're in bondage, like we're trying to earn what's already been given. When we don't understand the depth of His grace and the finality of the cross, we look elsewhere for purpose, belonging, and validation.

As Spirit-filled believers, we have God's Spirit within us, making it easier to follow Him. The Holy Spirit is our compass, our guide, our Comforter, leading us into all truth.

We need to understand that we are forgiven of past, present, and future sins. We are the righteousness of God! We've been delivered, saved, and healed. We need to remind ourselves that He created us for a purpose and has provided all that we need to fulfill that plan. So, with this in mind, the natural outcome should be a desire to stay close, to remain hand-in-hand with Jesus.

The second reason we sway in our dance with Christ is because we're not truly grounded in the Word. The Word of God is everything. It's our foundation. It tells us who we are, what we've been given, and what God has promised. It's like a mirror, reflecting our true identity in Christ and reveals the incredible grace we've received. And it's all good news. We need to invest time to learn His truth and His ways.

Why?

But the truth is that most people don't really read the Word. Almost everyone owns a Bible, but it often just sits on a shelf. And when they do read it, they may skim over it or treat it casually, not realizing the power it holds. It's not rooted in their hearts. It hasn't become their foundation, but rather a supplement.

Without the Word as our anchor, we're easily swayed. We start dancing to other rhythms. We lose our sense of direction. That's why being grounded in Scripture is vital, it keeps us hand-in-hand with Christ and helps us move in step with Him.

The third reason we sway from God in our dance with Him is because we're not spending intimate time with Him. There's no quiet time. No stillness. No space for just being with the Lord. And yet, everything—our strength, our direction, our peace—should flow out of that intimacy with Him.

The truth is that many Christians see intimacy with God as a task, as work. But it's not. It's a gift. That desire to be close to Him? It's already inside of us. God placed it there. We were made for fellowship with Him.

The Dance

But life gets loud. We get busy. And slowly, that quiet time fades. It's not that we stop loving Him, it's that we stop lingering with Him. But we need to return to enjoying Jesus intimately. Not just knowing about Him, but sitting with Him, talking with Him, listening to Him. That's where real connection happens. That's where the dance becomes beautiful again. He says to you, "I already love you. I know you. I want you to know Me. I want us to be so close and intimate that you hear Me, but you won't hear Me unless you're still and listening."

These things aren't about earning something, they're about responding to the love we've already received. But that doesn't mean we don't practice. It doesn't mean we don't set time aside to worship Him. Just like in a real dance, we have to move with intention, not to get a reward, but because of the relationship.

My husband and I like to take cruises. Whenever we do he asks if he and I could learn some dances before the trip. I am great dancing by myself and so is he, but we needed some practice dancing together. I would always say, "Yeah, yeah, when I get some time, but right now I'm pretty busy so maybe we can learn it on the cruise." That rarely happens. We struggle with the couple's dance. I admit I did not realize how important it was to him until our last cruise, and I heard some music I just had to dance to, but when I grabbed his hand and pulled him out there, we bumbled and fumbled a bit until we both got slightly frustrated. We hadn't prepared.

Spiritual preparation is important. Just like a dancer prepares before stepping onto the floor, we also need to be spiritually prepared for what's ahead. And part of that preparation is spending time in the Word and in worship, building intimacy with the Lord. It's not about fear or expecting something bad to happen. It's about gaining strength, clarity, and peace for whatever does come, because God already knows what's ahead, even when we don't.

That time in His presence anchors us. It strengthens us. It prepares our hearts so that when life moves, whether in joy, challenge, or change, we stay in step with Him. That intimacy becomes our inner stability. Our quiet confidence. Our source of real strength.

Chapter 6

Called to Make a Difference

As Christians, we are not called to be passive. We're not meant to just sit back and watch the world go by. We are called to make a difference. The Bible says faith without works is dead (James 2:17), and that applies not just to our personal walk but to our role in society.

We can't afford to be lazy Christians, sitting comfortably while darkness gains ground. We are called to stand for what is right, to speak truth, and to get involved, starting right here in our local communities.

That means showing up. That means getting involved in local elections, promoting and supporting Godly, moral candidates. It means making phone calls, knocking on doors, volunteering, and doing the work, because if we don't, who will?

Our church has already taken steps. We got involved in school board races, city commission meetings, and other community efforts. We prayed, we worked, and we saw the fruit of it. I'm proud of what we've accomplished, but we can't stop now. There is more to do.

Whatever God has called you to in the political realm, do it. Maybe He's calling you to run for office. Maybe He's calling you to support someone who will. Or maybe your calling is to teach, to lead worship, to disciple others, to reach people for Christ. Whatever it is, do it with all your heart (Colossians 3:23).

This ties into the vision of the Seven Mountains of Influence, the seven spheres of society where Christians are called to take ground for the Kingdom of God:

1. Family – Raise Godly children, build strong marriages, and restore broken homes.

2. Religion (Faith) – Preach the Gospel, disciple others, and keep the church pure and powerful.

3. Education – Teach truth, influence curriculum, and bring Godly principles back into our schools.

4. Government – Run for office, support righteous policies, and be a voice for justice and righteousness.

5. Media – Speak truth, challenge lies, and shine light into culture through news and communication.

6. Arts & Entertainment – Use creativity to glorify God, bring beauty, and confront cultural darkness.

7. Business – Lead with integrity, bless others through entrepreneurship, and use wealth to advance the Kingdom.

God has called us not to escape culture, but to transform it. He's looking for believers who will rise up in every mountain, every area of influence, and bring His truth, His love, and His righteousness to a world in desperate need.

So let's step up. Let's be bold. Let's be active. And let's do our part to bring God's Kingdom here on earth, as it is in heaven.

Chapter 7

Let's Enter In

You're invited to The Dance! He created you and knows you perfectly and intimately. Doesn't it make sense that we would want to dance with the One we're most intimate with?

He knows you better than anyone. He set you up within a specific boundary and habitation where you can commune with Him daily. Doesn't it make sense that you would want to dance with the One who knows you best?

The dance is fun. It's intimate. In dancing, we learn to flow together. It takes time, training, and commitment, and many never learn to dance because they just won't commit. Could it be they don't realize the value? Or, maybe they have other priorities? Learning to dance is not difficult and it's certainly worth it!

The Dance

This dance with Jesus is full of joy, purpose, and intimacy. It's the way we were created to live, step by step, hand in hand with the Savior. Yes, the enemy is always trying to lure us away with distractions and temptations, pulling us toward a different rhythm, but in the end we have a choice. And choosing to stay with Jesus, choosing to keep in step with Him, is always the best way!

The following are some Scriptures that spoke to my heart during this season of the dance. I pray they speak to yours as well and help you stay in rhythm with the One who leads us in love, truth, and victory.

Trust in the Lord with all your heart, and lean not on your own understanding; in all your ways acknowledge Him, and He will direct your paths.

Proverbs 3:5-6

Commit your way to the Lord; trust also in Him, and He will bring it to pass.

Psalm 37:5

Set your affection on things above, not on things on earth.

Colossians 3:2

Let's Enter In

Trust in Him at all times; you people, pour out your heart before Him; God is a shelter for us. Selah

Psalm 62:8

The fear of the Lord is the beginning of knowledge, but fools despise wisdom and instruction.

Proverbs 1:7

But whoever listens to me will dwell safely, and will be secure from fear of evil.

Proverbs 1:33

Let your eyes look right on, and let your eyelids look straight before you. Ponder the path of your feet, and let all your ways be established. Do not turn to the right or to the left; remove your foot from evil.

Proverbs 4:25-27

Since we live by the Spirit, let us keep in step with the Spirit.

Galatians 5:25

PART 2

Angie Buhrke

Chapter 8

Hopscotch Christianity

Since the day I said yes to Jesus, I've realized something: this life, this walk of faith, can be somewhat of a dance. But here's the question I've had to ask myself over and over again: Whom am I dancing with? Because every day, we all have a choice. Will I dance with God, and let Him lead me with grace and truth? Or will I fall into step with the enemy's lies, or follow the rhythm of a world that doesn't know where it's going?

The truth is that too many of us, myself included, have danced in and out of the Kingdom throughout our days. We love God. We're saved. That part is secure. But our thoughts? Our words? Our actions? They jump between faith and fear, trust and control, obedience and self-preservation.

It's what I've come to call "Hopscotch Christianity." One moment we're standing on Kingdom ground,

The Dance

believing, trusting, submitting. The next moment, we're standing in self-doubt, anxiety, gossip, and avoidance. We jump from square to square. God on Sunday, fear on Monday, faith on Tuesday, gossip on Wednesday, self-doubt on Thursday. We move in and out, convinced we're still in sync with God, and sometimes, we're not even aware we've stepped out of rhythm. We seem to hop in and out of the Kingdom life.

So how do we actually dance around God? Let me give you a real-life example. Let's say the Holy Spirit nudges you, clearly tells you to talk to your neighbor about Him. Not to just be nice. Not to drop hints. To actually speak to her about Jesus. You feel it in your spirit. You know it's Him.

But the moment comes, and you freeze. You don't like the person all that much. You're afraid of how they'll respond. You don't want to be rejected, embarrassed, or misunderstood. So instead of obeying, you start dancing around the instruction.

You pray for them instead. That's good, right? You invite them to church or Bible study. That's spiritual, isn't it? Maybe you even bake them something and leave a kind note. All great things. But deep down, you know you're avoiding what God actually asked of you. You're not dancing with the Lord. You're dancing around Him.

And then we go even further. We start dancing with other partners. We dance with fear. We dance with memories of the last time someone shut us down. We dance with our past failures, our insecurities, our worldly logic. We start moving to the rhythm of our own carnal reasoning instead of the voice of the Spirit. All the while, we convince ourselves we're being faithful, when really, we're just being fearful. This is where we need to pause and ask: Am I moving with God, or just moving near Him? Am I obeying, or am I avoiding?

Obedience isn't always comfortable, but it is simple. It's listening to His voice and saying yes. That's the dance He invites us into—not a performance, not avoidance, but a step-by-step following of His lead.

But here's the thing. As we grow in the Lord, we're not meant to live in and out of the Kingdom. We're meant to live *from* the Kingdom and to move in the Spirit. We're meant to stay in step with the One who leads with truth, even when it's uncomfortable.

The Dance

This book is written from a woman's heart, but its truth belongs to everyone. I want to say that up front. The gospel is for all of us, men and women. The call to an abundant life filled with peace and joy is for the entire body of Christ.

I will cover the sway of our thoughts, the beat of our words, the rhythm of our actions. I'm writing especially to those who've ever felt like they were twirling in confusion, stepping back in shame, or trying to find their footing again in the presence of a loving God.

This book isn't about judgment. It's about clarity. We can't keep choreographing our own steps and calling it God's dance. We are either dancing with Him through His instructions, or we're just spinning in circles, pretending we're moving forward.

I want to dance with Him through every instruction, every step of faith, every unknown. If you've ever felt like you're hopping from square to square, trying to figure out how to stay in step with God, this book is for you.

Let's find the rhythm of the Kingdom together. Let's keep in step with the King!

Chapter 9

New You = New View

Before we dive into the dance, into the thoughts, words, and actions that flow from our lives, I want to start by laying a firm foundation.

When we were born again, something radical happened. We became brand new. We were made clean. We were made holy, not by our own effort, but by what Jesus did for us. Our identity changed forever. Our sin nature was replaced with the righteousness of God.

In Christ, we are as righteous as Jesus is, not because of our performance, but because of His gift. We are as close to God as we'll ever be, because He now lives in us. Our hearts belong to Him, fully and completely, and He is madly in love with us!

This identity is the root. From this truth flows everything else. Yes, we'll talk about our thoughts, words, and actions, but those aren't just behaviors we try to fix. They grow out of relationship, out of intimacy with God. They are the fruit of knowing who we are in Him.

You know, I've always said that the way we view God is the way our lives will go. But I've come to realize, just as deeply, that the way we view ourselves is the way our lives will go also.

If we truly believed we are who God says we are, everything would change. The Word tells us we are new creations, not just patched-up versions of our old selves, but entirely new, through and through. It's like our spiritual DNA has been rewritten. The old is gone, and the new has come. That's not just poetry, it's reality. (2 Corinthians 5:17)

We are holy. We are righteous. We are beloved. All the things we think we're not, God says we are. And when we start to see ourselves the way He does, our lives will follow suit. Belief shapes reality. Identity drives behavior. So let's agree with Heaven about who we are, because our lives will always move in the direction of what we believe.

Let's take this further. James 4:8 says, *Draw near to God, and He will draw near to you.*

This isn't about physical distance. It's not like God is far away and waiting for us to come find Him. Scripture is clear. He said, "I will never leave you or forsake you" (Hebrews 13:5). He's not going anywhere. If you're born again, He's already living inside of you. You can't get any closer to Him than having Him in you.

So what does "draw near" mean? It's about intimacy, not geography. It means tuning your heart toward Him, becoming aware of His presence, opening up your soul to hear and respond. It's about engaging Him in relationship, not striving, but being still and aware.

And the truth is, He wants that closeness with you. But let's be honest, we often fill our lives with so much noise, so many distractions, that we crowd out the space where intimacy grows. We stay busy, distracted, overloaded. And in all that movement, we miss the whisper of God.

A few years ago, I had a dream that really stirred me. I didn't understand what it meant, but I felt like it was important. So I started asking God about it. But that week was incredibly busy. I was preparing for a big dinner event for pastors, and every day was full. Still, throughout the week, I kept asking, "Lord, what did that dream mean?" But I didn't hear anything.

Then, finally, the night of the event came. The dinner was over. The house was quiet. I was heading to bed, and for the first time all week, things slowed down. As I was walking to my bedroom, I thought about the dream again, and in that quiet moment, the Lord spoke. He gave me the first and last name of a man Al and I knew. That was it, just his name.

I was confused. I said, "Lord, he wasn't even in the dream. What does he have to do with it?" And God made it clear: "Absolutely nothing." He said, "Forget the dream. I just used it to get your attention. I need you to send some money to this man."

It hit me so clearly. God wasn't trying to teach me something through the dream. He was trying to reach me through my busyness. He used what He knew would keep me coming back to Him with questions, just so He could get a word in, so He could speak something on His heart.

That moment reminded me that God wants to speak. He is speaking. But sometimes, we're so full of activity, even good, ministry-minded activity, that we miss the gentle whisper. He'll use whatever means He needs to, just to draw us back into that place of intimacy where we can hear Him.

He's not far. He's speaking. But intimacy is cultivated in stillness, in attention, in choosing to slow down and draw near, not to get Him closer, but to experience how close He already is. If we want to keep in step with Jesus, we've got to pause long enough to hear His rhythm.

Before we move forward, settle this in your heart: You are clean. You are righteous. You are holy. And you are His. Get intimate with the One who truly loves you, and out of that intimacy, it will become clearer and clearer just how perfect you are in His sight!

Chapter 10

Backward Thinking

Now that we know who we are—clean, righteous, holy, and united with God—let's look at how that identity begins to shape how we live.

Colossians 3:12 says:

You are always and dearly loved by God. So robe yourself with the virtues of God, since you have been divinely chosen to be holy. Be merciful as you endeavor to understand others, and be compassionate, showing kindness toward all. Be gentle and humble, unoffendable in your patience with others. (TPT)

Did you catch that? You're always and dearly loved, and you're divinely chosen. Not because you're trying hard. Not because you're doing everything right. You're loved because you belong to Him.

The Dance

And because of that love, because we are already chosen, holy, and treasured, we robe ourselves with His character. We don't put on mercy and humility to earn His favor; we put them on because we already have it. Everything flows from the love and intimacy we have with Him.

We don't live to get closer to Jesus, we live *from* the closeness we already have. We walk in step with Him, not to earn love, but because we *are* loved. Let's continue with verses 13 through 17:

> *Bear with one another and forgive one another. If anyone has a quarrel against anyone, even as Christ forgave you, so you must do. And above all these things, embrace love, which is the bond of perfection. Let the peace of God, to which also you are called in one body, rule in your hearts. And be thankful. Let the word of Christ dwell in you richly in all wisdom, teaching and admonishing one another in psalms and hymns and spiritual songs, singing with grace in your hearts to the Lord. And whatever you do in word or deed, do all in the name of the Lord Jesus, giving thanks to God the Father through Him.*

Backward Thinking

We don't *have* to do these things. We *get* to do these things, all because we are already loved and divinely chosen as we saw in verse 12 at the beginning of this chapter.

We don't do all these things—love, forgive, show compassion, live holy lives—to get God to love us. We do them because He already does. We're not performing for approval; we're living from identity. We're not trying to earn something; we already have it. We're divinely chosen, not striving to be chosen. That changes everything.

There's a big difference between coming in the front door of a home and coming in the back door, and it says a lot about how we see ourselves in God's house.

When you come in the back door, it often means you're trying not to be seen. You're slipping in quietly, maybe feeling like you don't quite belong. Like you need to prove something before you can take a seat. Coming in the back door spiritually looks like striving, trying to earn love, earn acceptance, earn approval. It's a mindset that says, "If I just do more, pray harder, serve better, maybe then God will really love me."

But when you come in the front door, you come in like family. Like you belong there, because you do. You don't knock wondering if you're welcome; you walk in because love already opened the door for you. Spiritually, that's living from grace. It's knowing you're already chosen, already forgiven, already beloved, not because of what you've done, but because of who He is and what He's done.

Coming in the front door is living in response to love. Coming in the back door is trying to earn it. And here's the truth: God never asked us to sneak in the back way. The front door is wide open. Jesus is the door, and He already opened it through the cross. He welcomes us as sons and daughters, not servants trying to earn a spot. We don't have to perform for a place at the table. We already have a seat.

So let's stop trying to earn what's already been freely given. Let's stop living like guests in a house that's our home.

That's why Colossians 3 makes sense for us. We put on compassion, kindness, humility, gentleness, and patience, not to become beloved, but because we are beloved. We let the peace of Christ rule in our hearts, not to prove something, but because peace already belongs to us. We live differently because we are different. This is not performance. This is freedom. And freedom moves in love.

I felt it was important to pound this in, to really let it settle deep as the foundation for everything else we're going to talk about. Before we get into our thoughts, our words, and our actions, we have to get this straight: We don't live holy lives to get God to love us. We live holy lives because He already does.

Everything we do flows from identity. Our obedience doesn't earn us a place, it expresses the place we already have. We don't clean ourselves up to be accepted. We're accepted, and that transforms how we live.

So as we move forward, talking about how we think, how we speak, and how we act, never forget—we're not striving for approval. We're moving *from* love, not *toward* it. We're not trying to earn a "yes" from God. He already said "yes."

We are loved. Period. And because we are loved, we can live loved.

Chapter 11

Your Thoughts

There are three things that get us into trouble, but I want to give you the good news up front. You have control over every one of these issues.

It's funny. Everyone wants control. We're all control freaks in one way or another. And guess what? God actually gave us control, but not over others. He gave us control over our own lives. The problem is, we keep trying to take control of someone else's life instead of managing our own. Just know this: you have control over the three areas we're about to look at, and this is incredibly empowering.

1. Thoughts

Thoughts are the most powerful of the three. Why? Because everything you say and everything you do originates in your mind. It all starts with what you're thinking. That's why it's so important to become aware of what you're actually thinking about. Philippians 4:8 gives us guidance on how we should think and it's possible to actually think this way because God instructs us to do it:

> *Finally, brothers, whatever things are true, whatever things are honest, whatever things are just, whatever things are pure, whatever things are lovely, whatever things are of good report, if there is any virtue, and if there is any praise, think on these things.*

It's easy to think positively when life is going well, when the bills are paid, your relationships are peaceful, your health is strong, and your plans are working out. In moments like those, gratitude comes naturally. It's easy to smile, to thank God, and to feel confident about the future.

But what about when life isn't going so well. What happens when the job falls through, or the diagnosis is bad? What happens when the people you love hurt you, or when anxiety creeps in at night and won't let go? This is where the true test of our thoughts and our faith begins.

In hard times, our minds tend to default to fear, doubt, anger, or self-pity. And it doesn't help that the enemy loves to plant lies in moments of weakness:

- "God's not listening."
- "Things will never change."
- "You're not strong enough."

But here's the truth: you still have a choice. Even when life hurts, even when you feel overwhelmed, you have control over your thoughts.

This isn't just motivational talk, it's biblical truth. God wouldn't tell us to think on things that are true, noble, right, pure, lovely, and praiseworthy unless it was possible. But notice: it's not automatic. It's intentional.

Choosing to think God's way, especially in hard seasons, takes spiritual maturity and discipline. It requires you to catch yourself in the middle of a spiral and say, "No, I'm not going to let fear or negativity take over. I'm choosing to trust God's Word instead of my feelings." And Jesus gives us the perfect example of this. Look at John 13:1:

Now before the Passover Feast, Jesus knew that His hour had come to depart from this world to the Father.

Jesus knew. He was thinking. He was thinking about three specific things:

1. His hour had come.
2. He was leaving this world.
3. He was going to the Father.

Jesus knew what was coming. He understood what was about to happen to Him. And what He was facing wasn't pretty. I'm sure He had the opportunity to feel fear.

Remember Hebrews 4:15. Jesus was tempted in every way that we are. Why? Because although He was fully divine, He also came to earth as a human. He laid aside His divinity and operated as one of us. He wanted to show His disciples, and us, how to live in full dependence on the Father.

Jesus came as the Son of Man. That means He could have feared. I'm sure He felt the emotion of fear. But here's the key: it's not about whether you feel fear, it's about what you do with that fear.

Jesus felt fear. He was tempted to give in to fear. But He didn't. And in that, He showed us what's possible when we take control of our thoughts and submit them to God. Let's continue with verse 1:

Your Thoughts

Having loved His own who were in the world, He loved them to the end.

Jesus continues to think. He is thinking about His disciples whom He would love forever. He was protective and concerned for them as He knew they wouldn't take His death well.

It's kind of like a mother who finds out she has a serious illness. The first thing she thinks about isn't herself, it's her kids. She worries about how they'll handle it, who will take care of them, and how they'll go on without her. In the same way, when Jesus knew He was about to die, He wasn't just thinking about His own suffering. He was thinking about His disciples, His closest friends. He loved them deeply and was worried about what would happen to them after He was gone. That's why He spent those last moments teaching them, comforting them, and praying for them, because He loved them like family. Now let's continue with verse 2 as Jesus is still thinking:

Now supper being concluded, the devil had put into the heart of Judas Iscariot, Simon's son, to betray Him.

The Dance

Jesus' thoughts now turn toward Judas, His betrayer. How He must have felt. Deeply grieved, I'm sure. The Scripture tells us that Jesus knew who would betray Him (John 13:11), yet He loved Judas deeply just like the other disciples. Jesus was fully human and feeling sadness would have been natural.

Imagine loving someone, sharing life and ministry with them for years, and then realizing they're about to turn you over to your death. That would cut deep. So yes, Jesus could have felt heartbroken or disappointed. But His heartbreak wasn't about what was being done to Him, it was what Judas was doing to himself! He was sad for Judas!

His love wasn't fake, he really did love Judas, and that love made the betrayal even more painful. And yet, Jesus still chose to love, even knowing the pain it would bring. That's a powerful example of grace under deep emotional pressure.

These thoughts are heavy, not self-centered, but full of love and concern for others. They reflect Jesus' character: compassionate, purposeful, and deeply relational.

So, the key question becomes: What did Jesus do with His thoughts that were obviously going downhill. They

Your Thoughts

were becoming toxic. How did He respond? What posture did He take in the face of fearful, wearisome thinking? Let's find out in the next chapter.

Chapter 12

Switch Your Thinking!

Before we see how Jesus handled His thoughts, let's recap what we know so far.

1. Jesus senses the end approaching. He knows His time on earth is nearly up. He's preparing to return to the Father, but that transition carries emotional weight.

2. He thinks of His disciples, not in fear for Himself, but in concern for them. He knows they'll be confused, hurt, and shaken. His sadness is for their coming grief and struggle.

3. Then His heart and mind turns to Judas, someone He loved, someone He had created for a purpose. And He grieves not the betrayal itself, but what Judas would lose by walking away from his calling.

The Dance

These thoughts are heavy, not self-centered, but full of love and concern for others. They reflect Jesus' character: compassionate, purposeful, and deeply relational.

So, the key question becomes: What did Jesus do with His thoughts that were obviously going downhill. They were becoming toxic. How did He respond? What posture did He take in the face of fearful, wearisome thinking? Let's continue in John 13:3-5 and watch Jesus make the change:

> *Jesus, knowing that the Father had given all things into His hands and that He came from God and was going to God ... (vs. 3)*

This verse is like a quiet turning point. Jesus had every reason to be overwhelmed emotionally and mentally. He was carrying the weight of betrayal, separation, suffering, and the burden of those He loved. But here, he made a conscious choice to anchor himself in truth.

He remembered something:

- Who He was - the Son of God.
- What He had - all authority and power.
- Where He came from - the presence of the Father.
- Where He was going - back to that glory.

Switch Your Thinking!

Jesus switched His thinking on purpose! He changed His thought pattern. Jesus didn't suppress his thoughts, He redirected them. He took the downward spiral of grief and heartbreak, and turned it upward by remembering eternal truth. That mental shift became the fuel for the next action: serving in love, right in the face of death. This moment models something deeply practical and spiritual for us—that truth remembered can realign our emotions and empower our purpose.

And what's so striking is what He does right after recalling these truths: He takes on the role of a servant. He continues the will of His Father. He washes His disciples' feet. That's not just humility; it's intentional, empowered humility. Not weakness, but strength under control:

> ...rose from supper, laid aside His garments, and took a towel and wrapped Himself. After that, He poured water into a basin and began to wash the disciples' feet and to wipe them with the towel with which He was wrapped. (vss.4-5)

Jesus also focused on the joy ahead. He knew the pain wasn't the end. He saw what would come because of the cross—that we would be saved, and brought into God's family. That thought gave Him strength.

It's just like a woman going through pregnancy and labor. She's uncomfortable, sometimes even scared. But she keeps going because she's thinking about the joy of holding her baby in the end. That's what makes it worth it.

We were Jesus' joy. The thought of us being part of His family, living in His kingdom, made all the pain worth it to Him.

That's how Jesus handled all those hard thoughts, by remembering the truth and focusing on the joy ahead. And that gave Him the strength to keep loving, serving, and going to the cross.

Our thoughts matter. If we choose to dwell on fear, disappointment, or pain for too long, without filtering them through truth, we open the door to depression, anxiety, and spiritual paralysis. The longer we sit in those negative thoughts, the more toxic they become. Eventually, they can keep us from walking in the purpose God has for us.

It's not just about feeling bad, it's about what we're focusing on. When we let those harmful thoughts stay, we're not just wrestling with them, we're dancing with them. And if we're dancing with negative thoughts, we're dancing around the truth, and ultimately, we're dancing with the enemy. But Jesus gave us a model: switch your thinking on purpose.

- Remember who you are in God.
- Remember His promises.
- Focus on the joy set before you.
- Let truth guide your mind, not feelings or fear.

When we line up our thoughts with God's Word, that's when freedom comes. That's when purpose is unlocked. So, get back onto the dance floor with Jesus. There are plenty of good things to focus on!

Chapter 13

The Creative Power of Words

Words are not just sounds or syllables. They are seeds. Every time we open our mouths, we're either planting seeds of life or seeds of death. Proverbs 18:21 puts it plainly: *Death and life are in the power of the tongue, and those who love it will eat its fruit.* That means whatever we speak, we'll live in it.

From the beginning of time, God modeled the power of the spoken word. He didn't build the world with His hands, He built it with His mouth. He spoke, and it was. "Let there be light." And light didn't hesitate.

We were made in His image, and the same creative force rests within us. Our words can build marriages or break them. They can raise children in confidence or crush them under criticism. Words can shape destinies or sabotage them. They don't disappear when they leave our lips. They go to work.

The Dance

I'll never forget a night my husband and I were in North Carolina, dining out with a group of friends. The men were at one table, and the women at another. It was one of those long nights where nothing seemed to move quickly as service was slow, delaying the food.

Out of frustration or maybe just trying to lighten the mood, my husband said, "We're not going to eat until 8 PM." He wasn't making a prophecy, at least not intentionally. But do you know what happened? Everyone else at the table got their meals around 7 or 7:30. But my husband? 8:00 on the dot. It hit me: his words went ahead of him and arranged the schedule.

It may seem small. A dinner order, a passing comment. But the truth is, the spirit world is listening. Circumstances respond to sound. Your words are either commanding delay or releasing breakthrough. You're either inviting peace or giving access to chaos. You're either dancing with Jesus or dancing with the enemy.

Let's go deeper into the Word by looking at James 3:5–6:

> *Even so, the tongue is a little part of the body and boasts great things. See how great a forest a little*

fire kindles. The tongue is a fire, a world of evil. The tongue is among the parts of the body, defiling the whole body, and setting the course of nature on fire, and it is set on fire by hell.

That's strong language. Scripture isn't subtle here. The tongue can set the course of our entire life. One small spark can ignite a whole forest. James uses the imagery of fire. And to build a fire, you start with kindling. These are dry, thin pieces of wood, useless on their own, but when gathered together and sparked, they burn fast and hot.

Let's look at a modern example. Let's say it's Monday morning. You wake up, and the first thought in your mind is, "I'm tired." That might feel like honesty, but it's your first stick of kindling. You speak it out loud: "I'm tired."

Later that morning, your energy is still low, and you say again, "Man, I'm just dragging today." Second stick.

Then by lunchtime: "I can't wait to crash after work. I have no energy." Third stick. Before you know it, by 4:00 PM, you've declared: "Every day around this time, I feel like I hit a wall." Now you're building a fire with your own mouth.

The Dance

Then you call a friend and unload: "Girl, I've just been so off lately. Every single day I wake up exhausted. I must be getting old. Maybe something's wrong."

At that moment, you've taken a match and lit the pile. That little collection of words, those repeated negative confessions, turns into a blaze. And here's the danger. You're not just describing your life. You're directing it.

You're dancing around the truth, not in it. You've stepped out of rhythm with God's Word. And here's why:

- The facts might say: You're tired.
- The truth says: By His stripes you were healed. (1 Peter 2:24)
- The fact may be: You have symptoms.
- The truth says: The same Spirit that raised Jesus from the dead dwells in you and gives life to your mortal body. (Romans 8:11)

Now here's the spiritual reality. The enemy listens. He sees your words as open doors. When you keep declaring defeat, fatigue, or fear, you're giving him permission to drop a log on that fire. Now it's not just tiredness. You can't get out of bed. You're dealing with anxiety. Maybe even depression.

The Creative Power of Words

You go to the doctor, and they can't find anything wrong, because physically, maybe there isn't anything wrong. But the words you've sown may have created a spiritual and emotional weight that medicine can't treat. And now, side effects from medication can leave you worse than before. Not every issue is caused by our words—but many are.

Let me be clear: I'm not saying symptoms aren't real. I'm not telling you to ignore medical advice. But what I am saying is this—we must learn to agree with God's Word more than our feelings. Feelings change. God's Word doesn't. Symptoms shift, but truth stays.

When you wake up tired, you don't have to lie. But instead of saying, "I'm so tired," speak this: "Lord, I thank You that Your strength is made perfect in my weakness. I may feel tired, but I receive Your strength today. My body is energized, and my mind is alert. The joy of the Lord is my strength."

Now you're not throwing sticks on a fire—you're pouring water on it. You're shutting the enemy out and letting the Spirit set your rhythm for the day.

Let me ask you this:

The Dance

- What are you creating with your words?
- What realities are you reinforcing with your speech?
- Have you been speaking frustration over your life - or faith?

You don't have to accept everything that comes to mind. Not every thought deserves to become speech. Speak what you want to see, not what you fear will happen. Speak what you want, not what you have.

When we align our words with God's Word, we are moving in step with Him, we are dancing in harmony with the Spirit. His Word becomes our rhythm, our lead, our guide. But when we speak words of fear, doubt, and unbelief, we step out of that divine dance. We're no longer following God's lead. We've turned and started moving with the world, and even with the enemy. Because the devil can't take your authority, he will try to use your words to gain access. So, every word we speak is either an agreement with Heaven, or a partnership with darkness.

The good news is this: we have the power to choose. And when we choose to speak life, truth, and God's promises, we step into alignment with Heaven and Heaven moves with us!

Chapter 14

Actions of Honor

Our actions reveal what we truly believe. It's easy to speak love, but love without action is just noise. In Romans 12:10, we're instructed to "love one another with brotherly affection; outdo one another in showing honor." This isn't just about kindness. It's about value. It's about recognizing the worth in others and treating them accordingly. Honor is not earned by perfection, it's given by grace.

My husband and I used to tip based on service quality. If the server was attentive, we tipped well. If not, we gave just enough. But over time, our hearts shifted. We realized that this isn't about performance, it's about honor. Now, we often double or triple tip, not because the service is perfect, but because we want to bless people. We want to treat others as valuable, whether they meet our expectations or not. That's love in action. That's honor.

The Dance

We have a group of friends we eat out with regularly, and something beautiful happens every time. We all try to pay the bill. Not because we're trying to impress anyone, but because we genuinely want to bless each other. Everyone's reaching for the check. Everyone's eager to cover the meal. Why? Because we honor one another. We may not agree on everything, and that's not even a concern. Agreement isn't the foundation of our fellowship, honor is. We recognize each other's value. We esteem one another above ourselves, just like the Word teaches. It's not about who's right. It's about who we're called to be: people of love, people of grace, people of action. And honor is one of the highest forms of love in action.

The next two chapters will be filled with every day, real-life examples, personal moments from my own journey, not to show you perfection, but to give a picture of what it looks like to live a life of honor. Because honoring others isn't just about being polite, it's a reflection of how we honor God. When we honor people, we're honoring the One who created them. And when we truly honor God, that honor will naturally overflow into how we treat others. The two are inseparable.

Actions of Honor

Before I go any further, I want to take a moment to highlight something deeply important and close to God's heart. The Bible speaks with clarity and conviction about the value of honoring those who labor in teaching and leading the Church. In 1 Timothy 5:17, Paul writes:

> *"Let the elders who rule well be considered worthy of double honor, especially those who labor in preaching and teaching."*

This verse reminds us that our pastors, teachers, and spiritual leaders are not just filling roles, they are pouring out their lives in service to God and His people. Honoring them isn't merely a suggestion; it's a biblical principle. We can show this honor in many meaningful ways—through words of encouragement, consistent prayer, acts of service, and even through financial support. Appreciation events, handwritten notes, or simply offering to help carry their burdens in practical ways can speak volumes. By honoring those who teach and lead us in the faith, we not only express gratitude but also align ourselves with God's heart for His shepherds.

Let's continue with more life experiences.

Chapter 15

The Proof Is in the Doing

It's time to share simple, yet powerful examples from my everyday life, because often it's in the small things that we either choose to honor others or fall short without even realizing it.

One day, I went shopping with a close relative, and we picked up quite a few items. As I was loading everything into the car, I noticed a box of tissues that I hadn't paid for. I told her, "I'll be right back," and she asked, "Why?" I explained that I was either going to pay for it or return it since it wasn't on the receipt. I chose to return it to the shelf and left the store.

What surprised me was that, after that moment, she didn't speak to me for two whole weeks. I couldn't figure out why, until the Holy Spirit showed me that my decision to return the tissue box had convicted her. To her, it was just 69 cents, but to me, it was about integrity. More

The Dance

than that, it was about honoring God, honoring the store, and honoring the people who work there or had stocked those shelves. It reminded me that living a life of honor doesn't just apply to church settings, it applies everywhere. Whether someone is a believer or not, every person deserves honor, and our actions, no matter how small, reveal the condition of our hearts.

A similar situation happened not long after. I had been at the grocery store and bought two blocks of cheese. When I got to my car and began unloading, I found them at the bottom of the cart and wasn't sure if I had paid for them. When I got home, I checked the receipt, and sure enough, they weren't on it. So I tucked the cheese in the back of the refrigerator, planning to return or pay for them the next time I went back to the store. But by the time I did, just two days later, someone in the family had eaten nearly both blocks. I had nothing left to return.

So when I went back to the store, I picked up the same two blocks of cheese again. When I got to the register, I asked the cashier to ring them up but told her I wouldn't be taking them. I just wanted to pay for what I had previously missed. She looked at me like I had two heads. I

The Proof Is in the Doing

explained the situation, and she paused, clearly trying to understand. Then she said gently, "Oh, you don't have to do that. It's fine." But I told her, "No, I want to pay for it." She saw I meant it, and with a soft smile, she rang them up and had someone return them to the shelf. As I walked away, she said something I'll never forget: "No one does that. I've never seen anyone do that."

It may have just been cheese, but for me, it was a matter of integrity, and a way of honoring not only the store, but more importantly, God. These small moments are where our faith lives and breathes. Honor isn't just about big public gestures, it's about the quiet decisions we make when no one is watching, or when it would be easier to walk away. That's the kind of life God calls us to live.

One evening, Al and I were out to dinner with another couple. As we sat down, the waitress mentioned that anyone with a veteran's card could receive 15% off their meal. The gentleman we were dining with happened to be a veteran and had his card with him.

After the waitress walked away, his wife turned to Al and said, "I actually have an extra veteran's card. I don't remember how I ended up with it, but I'm going to give it to you. You can use it and get 15% off too. Don't worry, they won't even check the picture."

Al and I smiled and politely declined, but she insisted. She offered again. And again. Finally, after the third or fourth time, I looked at her and gently said, "We don't live that way. It's dishonest." She leaned back in her seat, seemingly surprised that I said it so directly. But then, after a moment's pause, she nodded and said, "You know what? You're right." She put the card away.

I don't know if she ever offered it to anyone else again, but in that moment, she reconsidered. I know she meant well and was trying to be helpful, but for me, it was about something bigger than saving a few dollars. It was about honoring the restaurant, honoring the people who earned that benefit, and most importantly, honoring God.

One day, I was getting my hair done when I noticed that my hairdresser was using a very unique, lightweight, and powerful hair dryer. I'd never seen one like it, and I asked her about it. She told me the brand and where she got it. Curious, I went online later to check it out. The price? $565.

The Proof Is in the Doing

That was a lot of money for a hair dryer. But even more than the price, it looked like the item was only available for purchase by licensed hair professionals. It required proof or at least a phone call for approval. So I didn't pursue it. A few weeks later, back in her chair, my hairdresser mentioned that the company had changed its policy and now sold the dryer to the general public. I went back to the website, but even then, I still couldn't justify spending that much.

The next time I went in, I remember walking toward the salon and thinking, I just hope she doesn't offer to buy it for me at her discount. She could easily do that, use her license to make the purchase, and let me pay her back. Many people wouldn't think twice about it. But I do.

I don't have a license. I haven't earned the discount. Taking advantage of someone else's credentials to get a deal might seem harmless to some, but to me, it's just not honest. It's a small compromise, but it's still a compromise. To my relief, and to her credit, she never offered. She respected the line I had drawn in my heart. And I respected her even more for that.

The Dance

Because it's not just about a hair dryer. It's about integrity. It's about honoring the businesses we deal with. And ultimately, it's about living in a way that reflects the values I believe in, even when no one's checking.

Recently, Al was in the garden center at Home Depot, just looking around and chatting with one of the employees. As they talked, he shared something that really stuck with Al. He said, "You wouldn't believe how many people, who come down to Florida for the winter, buy garden tools, shovels, rakes, brooms, and other items they need for a few months, and then, before heading back north, they return everything they used and get their money back.

He wasn't just talking about unused items. These were tools that had been used all winter long. And here's the thing: they're not breaking any store policy. Technically, they're "allowed" to return the items. But just because something is permitted doesn't mean it's right. It's dishonest. It's taking advantage of a generous return policy. And it puts a burden on the store and ultimately on other customers. Lack of honor, for sure.

Hearing that broke Al's heart a little, not just because of what it says about how some people view businesses, but because it reveals a deeper truth: when we compromise our integrity in small things, it becomes easier and easier to justify bigger compromises. Doing what's right isn't always convenient. But it always honors God, and it always leaves a lasting impact, on us, on others, and on the world around us.

The Bible says in 1 Samuel 2:30: *"Those who honor Me I will honor."* Honoring God isn't just about what we say, it's about how we live. It's shown in the small decisions, the quiet moments when no one else is watching, and especially in how we treat others.

When we honor people with honesty, respect, and integrity, we are honoring the One who created them. And when we live our lives out of a genuine relationship with God, honoring Him becomes the natural overflow of our hearts. It works both ways: when we choose to honor others, we reflect God's character. And when we walk closely with Him, our lives begin to naturally reflect that same honor in everything we do. That's a life that brings glory to God, and one He promises to bless.

Chapter 16

In Step with the King

Throughout life, we are always in motion, moving in rhythm with someone or something. The question is: Whom are we dancing with?

Sometimes we dance around what God has clearly spoken, hesitating to obey in our thoughts, compromising in our words, or justifying questionable actions. We pick and choose which steps we'll take and which we'll avoid, treating obedience like a buffet instead of a calling.

But following Jesus is not about choreography we perform on Sundays; it's about the everyday rhythm of life. It's in how we think, how we speak, how we act, and how we honor others. Every choice is a step in a larger dance, and every step reveals whom we're keeping in step with.

Let me ask you something: If you were arrested for being a Christian, would there be enough evidence to

The Dance

convict you? Would your life speak clearly of who you belong to, by your love, your humility, your integrity, your honor?

Because here's the truth: You were made to dance with the King. He has chosen you. He loves you. And in Him, you are the righteousness of God. So don't get swept away by the rhythm of the world or the whispers of the enemy. Stay in step with the One who gave everything for you. The music of grace is playing, and you are always invited to dance with the King!

Prayer to Receive Jesus as Your Lord and Savior

This is where your new life begins! Once you receive His gift of salvation, you become brand new with the nature of God residing on the inside of you. To receive Jesus as your Lord and Savior and to become born again, simply pray the following prayer aloud:

Jesus, I am sorry for my sins. I believe You died for my sins and that God raised You from the dead. I receive Your forgiveness, and I make You the Savior and Lord of my life. Thank You for saving me.

Congratulations! You are now a brand-new creation. Your spirit man is forever changed:

Therefore if any man be in Christ, he is a new creature: old things are passed away; behold, all things are become new.

2 Corinthians 5:17, KJV

Prayer to Receive the Baptism of the Holy Spirit

God's desire is to empower you to live your new life. Jesus Himself was baptized in the Holy Spirit before He ever began His public ministry. If Jesus needed it, we need it as well (Matthew 3:13–17). This is a separate experience from being born again (Acts 8:14–17). Salvation saves; baptism in the Holy Spirit empowers.

The gift of tongues is immediately available to believers once they are baptized in the Holy Spirit (Acts 10:44–46). Speaking in tongues is simply the Holy Spirit praying God's will through you. Your part is to allow Him to do so.

There are many benefits to speaking in tongues:

1. It promotes spiritual growth and edifies us (1 Corinthians 14:2, 4).
2. It keeps us aware of, and enjoying God's love (Jude 20–21).

3. It produces rest and spiritual refreshment (Isaiah 28:11–12).

4. It helps us to give thanks well (1 Corinthians 14:17).

5. It releases revelation knowledge (1 Corinthians 14:18).

Paul said, "I thank my God, I speak with tongues more than ye all." Paul wrote two-thirds of the New Testament and spent three years alone with God in the desert, where he received wisdom and revelation knowledge by praying in tongues.

Speaking in tongues is vital in the life of a Christian. You must desire it, ask for it, believe, and receive it. To receive the baptism in the Holy Spirit with the evidence of speaking in tongues, pray the following prayer aloud:

Lord, I want to be empowered to live this new life. I know this is a gift from You, and I need it to live the abundant life You've promised me. Please fill me now with Your Holy Spirit with the evidence of speaking in tongues. Thank You for baptizing me. By faith, I fully expect to speak in other tongues as You give me the utterance (Acts 2:4). In Jesus' name. Amen.

Prayer to Receive the Baptism of the Holy Spirit

Begin thanking and praising God for baptizing you, and begin speaking the syllables He gives you. This is the language the Holy Spirit has given to you. To speak this language aloud is an act of your will by faith. God will never force you to speak—it will always be your decision. Enjoy your new personal, spiritual language as often as you like, and as you do, you will build yourself up in your faith:

But ye, beloved, building up yourselves on your most holy faith, praying in the Holy Ghost.

Jude 20

Suggested Readings

Books by Todd Mozingo

Available on Amazon

Reviving Love

It's time to Revive Love. The Real Kind. The Kind That Changes Everything. Love isn't weak. Love isn't passive. Love isn't just a feeling.

The love of God is fierce, unshakable, and packed with supernatural power - but have we settled for a watered-down version? Have we lost sight of the Gospel's raw, transforming force? This book is a wake-up call. A charge to return to the love that rejoices in truth, endures all things, and never backs down.

The Five-Fold Framework

What if you were designed to be the way you are because Jesus had a purpose for you to fulfill in the church body? What if the reason you see things differently is because you were designed to see things differently? What if you understood that other people see things differently than you because they were designed to see things differently than you? What if we all figured out who we were designed by God to be and then realized that we all fit together to create an amazing picture in the Kingdom of God!

Holy Spirit Vindication

The Holy Spirit causes too much trouble in church today. He tends to make things get emotional and out of control. Right? So maybe the best thing to do is to shut Him down and make Him take a back seat. Why has the church decided that He is too complicated for people to understand? When something is right, reasonable, and justified, we will fight for it. Isn't the Holy Spirit a right, reasonable, and justified Presence? It's time for the church to fight for the presence of the Holy Spirit. It's time to vindicate the Holy Spirit.

Suggested Readings

Get it Together

Marriage can be one of the most difficult relationships in life! We approach it initially with excitement and great hope for the future. Then life happens and the struggles begin. But if Christ is the bridegroom of His church, then how was this thing called marriage supposed to work? Did God set up a relationship called marriage that can actually be a long lasting, loving relationship? In Get It Together we go straight to the Bible and discover the God has a plan that leads to a joy filled, amazing relationship with our spouse.

Books by Al and Angie Buhrke

Available on victorylifeministries.org and on Amazon

God's Discipline is Not What You Think!

Guilt. Shame. Fear. Many believers live under a weight they were never meant to carry, believing that God is angry with them because of their sin. But what if that's a misunderstanding of God's heart? What if punishment and discipline aren't the same thing? In this liberating and eye-opening book, you'll discover that the punishment for sin has already been fully dealt with at the cross. What remains is not condemnation, but loving correction from a Father who is for you, not against you. Step into the truth of your secure position in Christ, and find out what God's discipline truly is—it may surprise you.

Why Be Sick When You Don't Have to!

Do you know that, if you belong to Jesus, you don't have to get sick, stay sick, or even die sick! Al and Angie share the truth that it is always God's will to heal. As you read this book, you will discover truths that will transform your thinking, bringing healing into your life.

God Wants to Reward You!

God is a rewarder and He wants to reward you, both on this earth and in heaven. This book reveals personal revelation that Al received on exactly what these rewards are and how we can be sure that we will receive them.

Suggested Readings

Get Rid of That Anxiety with God Right by Your Side

Anxiety is a serious disorder that affects millions of people around the world. Those who seek medical help are usually given tools to "manage" their anxiety, but rather than coping, you can actually be free from this harmful emotion. Angie Buhrke shares truths from God's Word that will put you on the path to victory over anxiety. And

you won't be alone—God will be right by your side. Get ready to be free!

Made in the USA
Middletown, DE
17 June 2025